The Little
of Role Play

by Melanie Roan and Marion Taylor
Illustrations by Mike Phillips

LITTLE BOOKS WITH **BIG** IDEAS

Published 2013 by Featherstone Education, an imprint of Bloomsbury Publishing plc
50 Bedford Square, London, WC1B 3DP
www.bloomsbury.com

ISBN 978-1-408-19506-2

A CIP record for this publication is available from the British Library.

Printed in Great Britain by Latimer Trend & Company Limited
10 9 8 7 6 5 4 3 2 1
This book is produced using paper that is made from wood grown in
managed, sustainable forests. It is natural, renewable and recyclable.

The logging and manufacturing processes conform to the environmental

**To see our full range of titles
visit www.bloomsbury.com**

Contents

Introduction

How often do we see children spontaneously play at shops, post offices, garages and vets? These are examples of transactional role play, in which services or goods are offered and accepted. They hold a real fascination for so many children. This is probably because they are familiar situations that children have experienced or observed in real life.

Transactional role play especially helps to develop language and social skills. It can provide the building blocks for storytelling and writing. It gives children the chance to practise and experiment with what they have observed and can help to develop creativity and learning across the curriculum.

The role play window is a simple way to stimulate and enhance role play and particularly to encourage transactional role play.

What is a role play window?
It is a window through which children interact.

This can be home made from a simple cardboard box (see illustrations) or it may already exist in your setting as a puppet theatre, house or shop.

Why a window?
When children see a window they want to communicate through it and make it part of their imaginative play. It helps them to define the roles they will play. It is a resource for a role play area that:

▶ supports children's **current interests**

▶ **particularly** incorporates opportunities to develop **communication**, **literacy** and **numeracy**

▶ facilitates learning for children from all **ages** and **linguistic backgrounds**.

How can the window enhance role play?
▶ The role play window immediately sets the scene for transactional role play. It changes any play area into a role play area; playing with pedal cars can become a car park with car park attendant; dressing up play might become a fancy dress hire shop; play with soft toy animals can become a vets. This creates a **language-rich** environment which encourages and extends communication between children.

► A role play window also provides many opportunities for developing **literacy**. It is a place for children and adults to display a variety of **signs and labels**, encouraging mark making and early reading. Transactions often generate **paperwork**; tickets, programmes, information leaflets etc. which children can make and write. For example, in the Appendix (page 73) there is a photocopiable passport and driving licence. These can be useful in a variety of role play situations:

▷ The **passport** in any travel scenarios; perhaps for continental train travel (See 'On the right Track' page 33) or a journey into Space. (See 'To boldly go...' page 66)

▷ The **driving licence** for any situation involving a vehicle, for example driving a bus (See 'The Wheels on the Bus' page 25) or hiring a car. (See 'Need a Car?' page 39)

▷ Both driving licence and passport can be presented at the window as a means of **identification**, perhaps when booking holiday accommodation. (See 'Have a nice stay' page 41 or for 'Click and Collect' page 63)

► Paper and **mark making equipment** can easily be incorporated into play on either side of the window. Furthermore, resources such as signs, labels and forms can be written in children's **home languages**. This is an opportunity to **involve families** in the life of the setting.

► The window provides opportunities to promote **mathematics** too; for example, by displaying prices on tickets and labels and through the children being involved in buying, selling and counting. Other aids to numeracy such as clocks and calculators can become part of the play.

► The window encourages **creativity**; children take on roles, act out narratives and work with others engaged in the same theme.

► The window is a **versatile** resource that allows **children to be in control**. As their interests change from drive through café to car wash, so can the labels on the window.

How to use the window

1. **Take inspiration from the children:** Follow their interests and allow them to take control of setting up the role play area. Involving them in decision making will boost their confidence and make them feel ownership of the activity. Generally their interests will stem from real experiences but allow scope for imagination and invention. If Mission Control decides there will be a chip shop on the next Apollo Space Shuttle, so be it. Use the situation as a stimulus for further discussion and provide resources that allow children to explore what space personnel really do eat!

2. The activities described in this book are those that commonly arise due to experiences children often have. They include suggested starting points. **Listening to children** and **observing their play should always be the place to begin**; if a particular theme arises, provide resources to explore and extend their interests in the theme; invite a speaker to visit; visit a setting with the children; provide photos, books, and stories or use online resources. Ask open questions to see what the children already know (often more than you expect).

3. **Take inspiration from your local surroundings** which the children can directly experience. Are there particular museums, parks or historic sites to visit? Is travel by underground, bus or ferry accessible?

4. **Set up the role play area:** Talk to the children about what might be in the role play area. Provide resources around the window that are as realistic as possible. Involve children and their families in resourcing the area. It is also a good idea to approach local businesses and traders for help. If the "real thing is not available many resources can be made from junk materials (See "Enhance Your Window"). When interests wane it is a good idea to store collected resources in a labelled box so that the theme can be revisited when interest is rekindled.

5. **Ensure that resources reflect the variety of cultures and lifestyles of the children in your setting,** from cooking utensils to costumes, so that children feel comfortable in familiar contexts and so that they can experience aspects of each other's lives.

6. **Continue to observe and listen.** As play takes new twists and turns, so different resources might enhance and revitalise the role play area.

7. **Talk about labels and signs:** Labelling the window together is a powerful activity. Use it to model how useful literacy is, to allow the children to experiment with and practise mark making and as an opportunity to integrate IT into your setting.

> ▶ What should the labels say?

> ▶ What labels have the children seen on visits to settings?

> ▶ How should the labels be made? Can the children make them? Scribed by the teacher? Printed using a word processing programme? Pictorial labels? Photographs of real labels? Be sure to incorporate children's home languages in labelling, involving families as much as possible.

> ▶ Have strips of paper/card available so that new labels can be made quickly and easily.

> ▶ It is also useful to have signs that crop up frequently to hand, such as 'Please Pay Here', 'Please Queue Here' and 'Welcome' in home languages. As children meet these in different play scenarios they will become familiar with what the print says.

> ▶ **Consider a second window:** Linking two role play areas more than doubles the play value; link a car park and a shop or a café and a garden centre to add a new dimension to play. Suggestions for links are included in the activities in the book.

8. **Consider having your window(s) outside or linked windows inside and outside.** Outside play suits many children and has been shown particularly to encourage boys to become more involved in play.

9. **Have fun together:** Playing alongside the children allows you to observe and assess, reflect and extend their language and model language that might be useful for the particular role play situation. Know when to step back, but also watch for opportunities to enhance learning across the curriculum.

10. **Record the role play:** Through photos, home-made books, pictures, stories, newsletters, recordings and displays. Share your play experiences with families.

Links with the Early Years Foundation Stage

Development Matters in the EYFS outlines the Characteristics of Effective Learning and what adults can provide to promote children's learning across all areas of the curriculum. The role play window is a particularly useful and stimulating resource in this context because it is flexible and open-ended; it can be made relevant to children's interests and it can be used effectively in both indoor and outdoor spaces. The role play window promotes learning in the three prime areas and four specific areas as follows:

Prime Areas

▶ **Personal, Social and Emotional Development:** The role play window supports children in making relationships by promoting co-operation and collaboration. Children will grow in self-confidence and self-awareness by engaging in activities which interest them; children can choose role play scenarios and make decisions about their play through the use of this resource. Role play also helps children to manage their feelings and behaviour in experimental and playful situations.

▶ **Communication, Language and Literacy:** The activities in this book all begin with 'Starting Points' which involve children in listening, thinking and discussion when planning their play. Imaginative role play also encourages children to talk about what is happening as well as using language to pretend when acting out

▶ **Physical Development:** Children will be involved in activities using large and small scale movement skills. Many of the role play activities outlined encourage children to be active and negotiate space. They will also learn to handle a variety of tools and equipment.

Specific Areas

▶ **Literacy:** The role play window will foster children's enjoyment of written language by giving them opportunities to read and write labels and signs for the window and engage in mark making within their chosen role play situations.

▶ **Mathematics:** The role play window encourages numeracy by introducing activities involving counting, recording numbers and exchanging money. A queue at the window will also promote positional language and ordering!

▶ **Understanding the world:** The activities outlined encourage children to visit different parts of their local community and represent these places in their role play. The different role play scenarios also provide opportunities to engage with and talk about technology.

▶ **Expressive arts and design:** Role play will always be enhanced by encouraging children to represent their experiences and play with a variety of media and materials. Role play inspires children to be imaginative and to develop storylines with other children engaged in the same theme.

Make your own Role Play Window

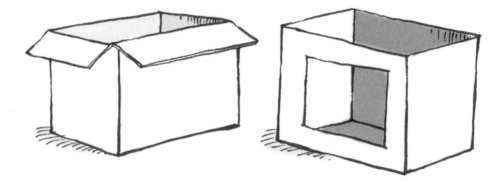

1. Take a large cardboard box.

2. Cut off the top flaps and cut a large hole in the front.

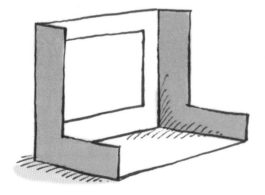

3. Cut out the sides and the back.

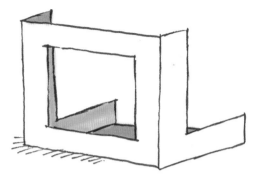

4. The window is ready to accessorise.

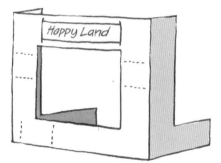

5. Cut slots for labels.

6. Make labels and accessories with the children according to their interests.

Now turn over for ways to enhance your window and adapt it for any role play situation.

Enhance your Role Play Window ——————————

Accessories for your window that will be useful in many role play situations

Once you have made your role play window, encourage the children to paint or embellish it.

You can customise your window to suit particular scenarios (as described in the activities sections) but the following additions are universally useful, enhance learning and make the window more fun to use:

Useful OUTSIDE (For the customer to view/use):

Open/Closed sign: A double sided sign to slot into your cardboard window slits or a piece of card folded lengthways to stand up with "Open" on one side and "Closed" on the other. Handy types might devise a window sign on dowelling that can swivel from "Open" to "Closed".

A clock and list of opening/closing times: Analogue (with hands that move) or digital; clipart or made by the children.

A numbered key pad: Children can enter a PIN code when making a payment, for example, and reinforce numeracy as they do so. To make a portable keypad that can be used by both customer and vendor, use a cheap or obsolete calculator. Add some card sides for secrecy. You can attach it to the window with a long piece of plastic covered wire (e.g. cut from an old phone) and duct tape.

A posting slot: In which to post credit cards, letters, messages, keys and no doubt a host of other items of the children's own devising. Children love to post things.

A bell: To ring for service. A small painted box with a red spot or bottle top to press can be attached to the window... or use a small hand bell for a more traditional establishment!

A phone handset: Not necessarily integral to the window but if a phone is available for the customer, they are sure to use it to talk.

Credit cards/money: for customers to pay for goods and services. Talk to the children about how their families pay for things. Show them real credit cards then design your own. Laminate small rectangles of card. You can add details that the children notice such as signature strips, shiny areas and long card numbers. Alternatively use clipart and laminate.

A dry wipe surface: for even more flexibility; for example when items or services are removed from a menu or when prices go up. This can be made by laminating a piece of paper and attaching it to the outside of the window.

For **money** use real coins. Bright shiny pennies work well. They can be cleaned with a pencil eraser, or soak them in a lemon juice/vinegar and salt solution but take care not to get it on fingers. This activity requires close adult supervision and risk assess the whole activity.

Table space and a pot of markers/paper (see below): for filling in forms or amending shopping lists!

Useful INSIDE (for the Vendor/Service provider to use):

Organise the items inside the window with labelled dividers or containers to store items tidily. Trays, shallow boxes or shoe box pigeon holes are all options, or you could make a desk tidy from junk materials.

Also useful are:

A cash till and a cash box: with cash for change (see above).

A calculator: for totting up bills, for example.

A keyboard and mouse: Use an old obsolete one or make your own from folded card (See "Click and Collect" page 63). This has the advantage that you can use either upper or lower case letters, reinforcing recognition of them.

Plenty of paper and mark making equipment:

Provide a variety of tools to make marks: Biros, marker pens, crayons, pastels, chalks and boards, pencils. The greater the variety the more the children will use them.

Provide different types of paper: Lined, squared, plain, small for quick notes, official looking forms. Attach clothes pegs (the squeezy kind) to the inside of the window to peg up small reminders. Post-it notes are especially popular and useful for quick messages and signs.

Some suggestions for paperwork relevant to particular scenarios are included in the activities which follow.

Other small stationery items: for example a hole punch (risk assessed), sticky tape. If you provide it the children will use it.

A phone handset: You can make a cradle for this, attached to the inside of the window, by cutting the top off a small box.

Table space: Ensure there is enough space for mark making and other activities, bearing in mind that more than one child might want to work behind the window.

Enhancements to the OUTSIDE of the Role Play Window

Enhancements to the INSIDE of the Role Play Window

Food on the Go!

Enhance your outdoor area with a Drive-through Café.

Starting points:

▶ Is there a nearby drive through restaurant you could visit?

▶ Talk to the children about their experiences of eating out. Have any had experience of buying food whilst in the car?

▶ Talk about what food they would like to serve in a drive through café. This is a good opportunity to discuss healthy choices. You can talk about savoury and sweet items and about the types of drinks they would like to serve.

Set up the role play window:

1. Staff can take food orders at the window. Provide a cash till and means of paying. Make pictorial order sheets showing choices, with tick boxes or numbers to circle beside each one. Draw a box at the top of the form for the order number, to be called when the order is ready.

2. Staff can pass the order forms to the chef and take payments from the diners in advance.

3. Diners can drive through in pedal cars or on trikes. Give them play money, credit cards and mobile phones.

4. Make and laminate menus so that diners can read and choose while waiting in the queue. Cut up photos of food, use children's own drawings or clipart.

5. Think about staff uniforms: Paper hats can be purchased at wholesalers, made (search Origami GI hat) or perhaps donated from your local drive through. Add cooking aprons with name badges.

6. A chef/chefs can prepare food in the kitchen area. Set up your play kitchen and equipment here. (Wholesalers sell empty boxes/bags to serve food in.)

7. Use play food or make food from dough. You might want to make your own pretend food. Make wraps from a circle of paper; fold and fill with coloured tissue paper or other collage materials. Make pretend ice creams and sundaes using the ideas in 'Ice, ice baby!' (page 47.)

8. Alternatively, use real food: Talk about the importance of hand washing and keeping food preparation areas clean. Children could design and make their own sandwiches, wraps and pizzas, incorporating snack time in their play. Concentrate on one food; perhaps a drive through fruit bar or a milk bar.

9. Ask diners to park their cars before collecting their food orders from an adjacent table. (see 'Park your Car', page 27).

10. Provide tables and chairs as an alternative to eating in the car.

11. Staff could also be responsible for clearing and cleaning tables. Provide cloths, water, bowls, trays or a trolley.

More little ideas:

▶ Talk about how food is stored. Why is some food kept in the fridge/freezer? Look at the real fridge and freezer in your setting and what is kept inside.

▶ Diners might phone in their orders instead of ordering at the window. You will have to warn customers not to use their mobile phones while driving! Staff can answer on the window's phone.

▶ Make hats or decorate caps as staff uniforms. Give your café a name and a logo.

▶ Provide a recycling bin for empty food containers so that they can be re-used.

Read all about it!

Promote early reading skills by setting up a kiosk selling children's magazines

Starting points:

▶ Talk to the children about their favourite magazines. These might reflect their interests, or favourite films or TV programmes.

▶ Think about making a bar chart or pictogram to illustrate this. Show the children how to collect and represent the information; begin by selecting a few different magazines and asking each child to put a token beside their favourite, count the tokens for each magazine and transfer these numbers to the bar chart.

▶ Encourage the children to bring in magazines to share with their friends at story time. Look at the picture stories together and involve the children in talking about the characters and the way the stories are sequenced, for example following the pictures and text from left to right. What other parts of the magazine do the children like? Gifts, puzzles and competitions are often popular.

▶ Have any of the children had experience of buying magazines at a station or airport to pass the time on a long journey?

Set up the role play window:

1. The role play window will be used to sell the comics. Add a cash till or cash box and a phone, and mark-making equipment for making orders and arranging deliveries.

2. Ask for donations of magazines from parents. Use sticky tape to reinforce the spines and cover the staples.

3. Involve the children in sorting the magazines according to titles or interest. Take their ideas, but be mindful of gender stereotyping.

4. Encourage the children to think about organisation; they could put out a limited number of magazines and stack the remainder in boxes in an adjoining 'store room' area.

5. Arrange the magazines on a bookshelf or table adding appropriate labels.

6. Think about prices, but keep your pricing policy simple! Make price labels for the shelves.

7. Display some recommended magazines under the banner headings 'Our Choice' or 'Often bought together.'

8. Cut and stick old magazines, draw or paint to make posters. These might advertise individual magazines or group titles according to themes. Display the posters around the role play window.

9. Consider using the Magazine Kiosk as a second role play area alongside a station (see 'On the right Track' page 33) or bus (see 'The Wheels on the Bus' page 25). If the kiosk is to be the primary role play area, simple rows of chairs set up to represent a train, bus, plane or ferry will provide children with a situation in which to read their magazines.

10. During play, an assistant might help to keep the stock tidy and replenish magazines from the store room as they are sold. The kiosk owner and assistant will need to tidy the shelves and cash-up at the end of play.

More little ideas:

▶ Place a noticeboard beside the kiosk for small ads, lost pets, local services and so on.

▶ Include magazines in the variety of reading material available to children in your Book Area.

▶ Add magazines relevant to the reading opportunities on offer in other play areas.

Let's play Post Office

Use children's experiences of a real Post Office visit in their role play.

Starting points:

▶ Encourage the children to write letters or draw pictures to send to their families at home. Have addressed stickers ready for the children to stick on their envelopes.

▶ Now visit a real Post Office. Risk assess and check your adult-child ratio first.

▶ Help the children to buy stamps at the Post Office counter and post their letters in the box. Apart from the counter services, what else is on sale in the Post Office?

▶ Talk about what will happen to their letters now; the sequence of posting, sorting and delivering the post.

▶ Encourage the children to track their own post by letting everyone know when it arrives!

Set up the role play window:

1. The role play window will form part of your Post Office counter. Provide a cash till and use the window to provide a range of Post Office services as detailed below.

2. Fill trays or shallow boxes with blank forms; collect real forms, use the photocopiable passport and driving licence forms on pages 73 and 74 and involve children in making their own documents using squared paper.

3. Provide stickers to use as stamps.

4. Don't forget that large letters cost more. Make a 'size guide' by cutting a slot in a piece of sturdy card. Post Office staff can test the size and thickness of the letters by passing them through the slot. They will need to charge more for letters that won't fit through.

5. Provide different sized boxes and brown paper for the children to make parcels. This will encourage problem solving; thinking about shape and size. Vary the weight of parcels by putting something inside. Include scales at the Post Office counter.

6. Have a table adjacent to the window selling stationery. Involve children in making Birthday cards to sell. Use a Paint program on your computer to print wrapping paper; there are programs available that allow children to paint a design, minimise it and repeat it over the page.

7. Encourage children to organise themselves into a queue in front of the window. Model ordinal language; first, second, third. Could you use a second window for busy days?

8. Provide a post box outside the Post Office area. Add a label with collection times.

9. To generate post, set up a writing table nearby stocked with the following resources:

    ▶ Plain paper, lined paper and coloured paper in different sizes.
    ▶ Greetings cards, notecards, invitations and postcards.
    ▶ A4 card for making own greetings cards.
    ▶ Envelopes in different sizes.
    ▶ A variety of pens and pencils.

More little ideas:

▶ Make a simple sorting office. Number some envelopes and match them to numbered shoeboxes.

▶ Use your Post Office play to celebrate festivals when cards are traditionally sent; Diwali, Passover, Hanukkah, Eid, Christmas and Easter.

Doctor in the house!

Set up a role play medical centre.

Starting points:

▶ A visit to a surgery is an ideal starting point.

▶ You might find a parent or carer with medical experience to talk to the children about their work.

▶ Talk to the children about their experiences of visiting the doctor. Discussion might include why they went, what the doctor did, how the doctor helped to make them better or keep them healthy (e.g. immunisations).

▶ Talk about appointments and waiting rooms and how a surgery might be laid out.

▶ Be sure to reinforce safety with regard to medicines.

▶ Some children might have experiences of hospitals. Listen sensitively and be sure to allow time for them to recount their stories.

Set up the role play window:

1. Use the role play window as the reception for the surgery. Provide an appointments book, mark making equipment and an old keyboard or laptop. Ensure that there are phone handsets both at the window and in other areas of your room so that appointments can be pre-booked!

2. If you have screens you could screen off an area/areas for doctors room/s (numbered) and the waiting room.

3. Add a whiteboard with the names of the doctors who are in surgery that day and their room numbers.

4. Provide doctor's kits for the doctors, together with clipboards and pens.

5. Talk about what sort of medical records you want to keep. Children might want to record facts about themselves and patients in booklets, zigzag books or on blank index cards.

6. Find suitable posters for walls/screens – ask at the surgery. Provide children's magazines, a small box of toys, chairs and tables for the waiting room.

7. Talk about how to stay healthy and make your own posters to encourage patients, with photos, collage or paint.

8. Toilet rolls provide hours of fun for patients who require bandaging!

More little ideas:

▶ Talk about baby clinics and together decide whether you want one at your surgery. If so provide dolls, baby equipment and a set of scales. The weight of the baby could be recorded in a booklet.

▶ An additional role play window can be used for a pharmacy. Provide small junk boxes and plastic bottles with lids. Think about designing simple prescription forms for doctors to fill in. Patients could take them to the dispensary to be prepared.

▶ Another role play window could be set up as an accident and emergency department in a hospital. Ride-ons with space for two make excellent ambulances, in cases where the doctor feels more treatment is needed. Pillows and duvets could be available for those needing an overnight stay.

Borrow a Book

Turn your book corner into a library.

Starting points:

LET'S BEGIN

▶ Visit a real library and choose some books.

▶ Talk about how the library works: borrowing books, enjoying them at home, how to take care of them and how to return them.

▶ Talk to the librarians about their jobs. How do they know where to find a particular book?

▶ Look at how the books are arranged. Depending on the children's level of understanding you could talk about story books (fiction) and books about real things (non- fiction), arranging books about the same subject together and, for those interested, alphabetical order.

▶ What else can you borrow from the library?

▶ Look at how the seating areas and displays are set out, how the computer is used and other services the library provides.

Set up the role play window:

1. Place the window on a table in your quiet book area. Set up areas labelled 'in' and 'out' on either side of the window for returning and borrowing books. Decorate the walls with story posters. Include different seating areas: comfy chairs, cushions and tables with chairs.

2. Use junk modelling materials to make a "scanner" to use when books are borrowed and returned.

3. Make library cards together: Decide on a name for your library; add a bar code, a strip for the child to sign their name and space for a photo or drawn self-portrait. Laminate the cards for use in play.

4. Add simple forms for ordering books and for reminding users that books are due for return.

5. Check that you have a varied collection of books and include books in children's home languages where appropriate.

6. Ask the children to help sort the books and put them in different areas. See what ideas they have following your visit. They might want to put all books about bears together, for example. Accept these ideas and make pictorial labels together for the different groups of books.

7. Make your own books to add to your library's collection. These could be mini books, giant books or zigzag books. First talk about the parts of a book: the cover with the title and the author's name; the pages with numbers, illustrations and writing; the blurb on the back. Then make your own books: individually using mark making; with an adult scribing, or as a group. Incorporate photos or the children's illustrations. Your first book might be entitled "Our visit to the library"!

8. Hold regular story telling sessions in your library led by children or adults. Provide props for favourite stories.

More little ideas:

▶ Work with parents to encourage children to join their 'real 'local library.
▶ Invite children to talk about their favourite books. Let children take turns to choose "Book of the Day" and display this.
▶ Add a magazine/comic section and an audio section where children can listen to story CDs.
▶ Make displays of collections of books, depending on the children's current interests
▶ Create book marks to sell at the library counter.

The Wheels on the Bus

Buy a ticket from the bus driver then take your seat.

Starting points:

▶ Organise a real trip on a bus to the depot. Try to organise for the children to buy their own ticket. (Choose a quiet time!) Take photos. Remember to ask for written permission from parents/guardians and risk assess. Alternatively...

▶ See if you can arrange for someone from a bus company to come and talk to the children.

▶ Show the children books/pictures/video of buses

▶ Ask about the children's own experiences of bus travel.

▶ Talk about what is inside the bus as well as outside and about the sequence of the journey; queuing, buying tickets, ringing the bell before your stop.

▶ Take the opportunity to talk about road safety and particularly bus safety: Wait for the bus to stop completely before you get on or off.

Set up the role play window:

1. Set up a rectangular table. This will represent the front of the bus. At one end place the role play window, at the other place the driver's seat. The window should face the passengers as they board the bus. For the other end of the table make a control panel with the children.
Make a steering wheel by attaching a paper plate to the centre of a box with a paper fastener. Add plastic bottle tops for buttons to press and label them pictorially and with writing e.g. "wipers". On the front of the box write the number and destination of the bus, following discussion. Two or more buses might be travelling to different destinations. Which number bus should you catch?

2. Add tickets and money. Talk about the difference between single and return tickets.

3. Add a phone handset to communicate with the depot.

4. Arrange rows of chairs behind the table with an aisle between. Tape a "bell" to the back of one chair, to press when passengers want to get off. Talk about leaving an area clear for wheelchairs and together make a sign. You might want space for passengers' shopping/pushchairs too.

5. Create a bus stop where passengers can queue. This is a good opportunity to reinforce ordinal language – Who is first, second etc.? Remember to let passengers get off before you board the bus!

6. If the driver's seat is the most popular you may need to create a staff roster to reinforce turn taking. Don't forget to check that your bus driver has the appropriate driving licence! (See photocopiable driving licence page 74)

More little ideas:

▶ Combine the bus with a café role play where staff can take their breaks or with a shop role play area to give passengers a purpose for travelling.

▶ Depending on the age of the children, create a very simple timetable. Is the bus on time?

▶ Use the opportunity for some "Bus maths": If there are two passengers on the bus and two more get on, how many passengers are there altogether?

▶ Have toy buses, cars and road mats available for small world bus play.

▶ You may need to employ staff to wash/valet the bus once it is back in the depot.

▶ Children might want to be inspectors, checking the tickets.

▶ Add a tool box in case the bus breaks down.

Park your Car

Plan and set up an outside car park for your ride-on vehicles.

Starting points:

▶ Car play on ride-ons is always popular. Making a car park would give this play a new dimension and purpose, involving some children who might otherwise not be interested in role play.

▶ Talk about children's experiences of using car parks with their families. What is the sequence or order of events involved in parking in a car park? Why are car parks needed?

▶ If there is a car park near your setting, think about who uses it and why. Take photographs of how the car park is set out to help you plan your own car park.

▶ Take the opportunity to talk with the children about safety in real car parks. Children should stay with an adult and beware of moving vehicles. Never play in a car park.

Set up the role play window:

1. The role play window will act as the entrance and exit to the car park; think about where to position it so that there is room for cars to drive in and out on either side.

2. Involve the children in planning the parking area: Count how many cars and bikes you have; how many spaces will you need so that each vehicle has a space? Talk about the flow of traffic around the car park. Will you need arrows?

3. Town planners often find it helpful to make a model first. Use toy cars and a piece of card cut to the shape of your outside area. Draw lines for the spaces, build the role play window from bricks and plan the way in and out.

4. Once you have decided on the layout, go outside and mark out the spaces with chalk or masking tape. Add arrows and the words 'IN' and 'OUT'. Place the role play window at the entrance. Consider making a barrier. (See 'Pay as you Go' page 31.)

5. Involve the children in designing and making tickets. Consider having short and long stay tickets with different prices. Laminate them to make them sturdy.

6. Cars can queue at the role play window, car park attendants can count/ calculate if there is a space and then issue a ticket. Drivers can pay at the role play window, or drop their coins into a washing up bowl or plastic box labelled 'coins' placed beside the window. Exact money please!

7. Drivers should park in the marked spaces and then display their tickets on their vehicles. On windy days tickets may need to be attached to the cars with sticky tape. Can the parking attendant help?

8. An attendant can patrol the car park checking tickets, making sure that cars are parked safely and issuing parking tickets.

More little ideas:

▶ Add your model car park to your small world car play.

▶ Link your outside car park to other role play areas indoors, for example a station (see 'On the right Track' page 33), art gallery (see 'Create an Art Gallery 'page 61) or shop, or simply park before going to play.

▶ Car park play will involve children in mathematical thinking and problem solving. Count cars and spaces; there are eight spaces in the car park and five cars have been parked, how many spaces are left? If three cars are parked on one side of the car park and two cars are parked on the other, how many cars are parked altogether?

Fill up with Fuel

Set up a garage and petrol station around your ride-on vehicles.

Starting points:

▶ If you have internet access watch the video of a real garage on http://www.teachfind.com/teachers-tv/early-years-role-play-pupil-programme-garage together.

▶ Arrange a visit to your local garage. Be sure to risk assess such a visit before hand. Try to look behind the scenes in the workshop and look at the petrol pump and shop areas. Talk about the different kinds of work that might go on (repairs to engines, tyres, brakes; MOT tests).

▶ Children might have their own stories to share about car breakdowns or garage visits. Can the any of them describe, from their own experience, the sequence of events when filling up with fuel?

▶ Perhaps members of the children's families have worked in a garage setting and could come and talk to the children in your setting.

Set up the role play window:

1. The window can be based in a shop and take payment for petrol and/or can provide bills for repairs etc. and a place to pay for them. Ideally have two windows. Provide cash tills, means of paying, clip boards and mark making equipment together with a diary for taking phone bookings. Mechanics may also need to give written estimates or order spares by phone.

2. Provide tools and overalls. See if you can source some real spare parts, old wheels or tyres for added realism. An old hosepipe can provide air for tyres. Risk assess props before use and supervise play closely.

3. Use your setting's bikes and pedal cars as vehicles or make your own from boxes (see 'Pay as you Go' page 31). An imaginary vehicle can even be built around a simple prop such as a steering wheel or paper plate.

4. Large weighted boxes and pieces of tubing will easily convert into petrol pumps.

5. Number your pumps so that drivers can report to the attendant which one they have used.

6. Talk about petrol and diesel. Can any children find out what they use at home? You may want to sell different types at your pumps and label vehicles with a "P" or "D" according to which fuel they should use. If a mistake is made a towing vehicle might need to be called in!

More little ideas:

▶ Combine this with a carwash role play area (See 'Need a Car' page 39).

▶ Develop the retail part of the garage depending on space and children's interests (provide shopping baskets, bags and goods to sell).

▶ You could secure small torches to vehicles to serve as lights. These would need careful checking during an MOT.

▶ To develop listening skills, check brakes by seeing how quickly children can stop their vehicle on a given signal (clap/bell/bang on a drum).

Pay as you Go

Introduce a toll booth and barrier to your vehicle role play.

Starting points:

▶ Has anyone ever been travelling in the car when it has to stop and pay to go further? Perhaps when going on holiday? Talk about charging on some motorways and bridges, or if relevant to where you live, congestion charges.

▶ A list of UK toll bridges can be found at http://www.igreens.org.uk/toll-bridges.htm so you can find the nearest to you that the children might have experienced. Print out some pictures from the website to show the children. Talk about how the cars are made to stop and the different ways they might pay.

Set up the role play window:

1. Set up the window on a table to be the booth. Include a cash till with change for cash payments and a bucket beside it for those who have the right coins to pay. Provide mark-making equipment to tally cars and always be ready to telephone the police if a motorist fails to stop or pay! Add a control panel for imaginary automatic opening and closing of the barrier (see below).

2. To make vehicles (or vessels for a river toll) use cardboard boxes with the bottom removed. Attach two straps (old tights are ideal) so that the vehicle can be stepped into and worn over the shoulders. Add paper plate steering wheels, bottle top lights and a number plate. Risk assess and supervise.

3. Set up a barrier. Plan with the children how to do this. Some possible solutions are:

▶ A row of chairs

▶ A row of cones

▶ For a movable barrier to be raised and lowered by the toll booth operator, use long strips of sturdy card attached together with a split pin and taped to the table. Attach one end to the table beside the booth using heavy duty adhesive tape.

Make sure these barriers are not at eye level and discuss safety rules with the children. Supervise the area.

4. You may want to introduce a multi-journey ticket for motorists who want to do a lot of journeys in a hurry. Write the numbers one to ten on a piece of card. The toll booth operator can stamp, colour or hole punch the ticket each time it is used.

More little ideas:

▶ Introduce a traffic light system (red and green cards labelled STOP and GO on either side of a broom handle) operated by another child.

▶ For a smoother traffic flow, have a second booth to allow more operators to be involved. Cordon off lanes for cash and multi-ticket holders, for example.

▶ Old school shirts can be easily modified to make uniforms for operatives. Add a pocket sticker with the operative's name and job title.

▶ Troll Bridge: Tell the story of 'The Three Billy Goats Gruff'. With the children's help, set up a bridge with large bricks or crates. Make masks or headbands with ears for the four characters. Including a toll booth will add an extra twist to the story!

▶ For extended play, add a petrol station (see 'Fill up with Fuel' page 30) and a café (see 'Food on the Go') to make your own motorway service station!

On the right Track

Make a role play station and train.

Starting points:

▶ Talk to the children about their experience of train travel and visiting stations. Discuss how to keep safe on stations and the dangers of playing near railway tracks.

▶ Look at images of big mainline stations online. Choose one that is nearby or that the children have visited. Is there anyone with experience of working with trains or on stations who could come and talk to the children?

▶ Some children are fascinated by trains and this is evident in their small world play and love of railway stories. Station role play would develop this interest further.

Set up the role play window:

1. The role play window might be used to sell tickets, reserve seats and give information to passengers in the form of timetables, maps and leaflets. Add a cash till, some means to pay, a phone and a clock.

2. Involve the children in making a range of tickets such as day tickets, family tickets and season tickets. Make seat reservation cards (simple number cards to match the numbered seats on your train). Help children to design, scan and print a train logo to use on tickets, timetables and station signs. Provide squared paper for children to write numbers on their own timetables. Look at real tickets and timetables for ideas.

3. Decide together about destinations for your train; perhaps your nearest city or a popular place for a day out or holiday. Think about making simple maps and information leaflets or collect real examples. Arrange these on a table alongside the window.

4. Decide on an area to represent the platform. Talk about the importance of accessibility for disabled passengers. Mark out the platform with masking tape and number it with a big number tile.

5. Make signs and displays for the station, including a whiteboard for departures. If possible, take photographs of the environmental print on a real station and show these to the children. Make posters advertising destinations or the pleasures of train travel.

6. Now build your train together. Use big building bricks or a large cardboard box for the engine. Add a destination board and perhaps your train logo to the front of the train. Use bottle tops on the control panel; red for 'stop', green for 'go' and other picture symbols for lights and wipers. Depending on the number of passengers, arrange about six numbered chairs behind the engine to form the carriage. Think about setting up a second carriage as a buffet car with a small table, or serve snacks from a trolley.

7. Set up a Waiting Room with chairs, books, magazines and a clock.

8. Station and train roles might include ticket office staff, a station manager to help passengers and check the platform for unattended bags, a train driver, a train manager to check tickets and seat reservations on board, and a guard to signal to the driver that the train is ready to leave. Train and station staff might wear high visibility jackets. Add stickers with job titles. Provide microphones for making announcements in the station or on board the train.

9. For the passengers, provide bags, luggage, baby dolls, soft toy pets in carriers and mobile phones (toys or old phones no longer in use). Encourage the passengers to develop stories about their journeys.

More little ideas:

▶ Extend your station by adding a café, left luggage department (see 'Lighten your Load' page 36), magazine kiosk (see 'Read all about it!' page 17) or hotel (See 'Have a nice stay!' page 41).

▶ Set up a car park alongside the station for 'Park and Ride' play (See 'Park your car' page 27).

▶ Think about creating another role play situation at your tourist destination. (See 'Happy Holidays!' page 43 for ideas).

▶ Adapt the station to be an Underground station if that is more relevant to children's experience.

▶ Access educational resources about track safety, including a song about safety at level crossings, at www.networkrail.co.uk/safety-education.

Lighten your Load

Set up a role play 'Left Luggage Point' together.

Starting points:

▶ Explore the meaning of luggage: items taken on a journey. Children's ideas might include prams and buggies, musical instruments, umbrellas, sporting equipment and, of course, all kinds of bags; shopping bags, rucksacks, suitcases, holdalls, beach bags..... Encourage the children to describe their own favourite bags.

▶ Point out that luggage can be awkward or heavy to carry around. Do the children have any experience of this?

▶ Explain that, during a break in the journey, to make things easier, luggage might be left at a Left Luggage Point to be collected later. Have any of the children or adults in the setting used a left luggage department before?

- Pictures of left luggage departments at various stations and airports are available to view online. Choose a location near you.

- Another starting point might be the identification of children with enclosure or transporting schemas who might be particularly interested in this kind of play. A child with an enclosure schema would develop their play and learning through filling up and emptying containers of all kinds, including bags. A child with a transporting schema might be absorbed in carrying objects, perhaps in a bag, from one place to another.

Set up the role play window:

1. Left luggage attendants will use the role play window to take in luggage from travellers.

2. Ask for donations of bags from parents to supplement your collection of luggage. Risk assess donations of luggage first and check that fastenings are safe for children to use. Remind everyone that plastic bags can be dangerous and should be kept away from children.

3. Provide a supply of blank luggage tags for travellers to encourage mark-making and name writing. Show the children how to make their own with card, a hole punch and string. Talk about home addresses and destinations to increase awareness of place.

4. During play, bags can be taken into the left luggage department over a table or counter set up beside the role play window.

5. Decide together whether you want to introduce a charge for the use of the service and, if so, add a cash till and some ways to pay. Will there be a higher charge for large items?

6. Involve the children in writing numbers on slips of paper; these will act as receipts for staff to issue at the window. Attendants can then label the luggage with the same number as on the receipt.

7. Encourage the children to devise a system for sorting and storing items, for example different labelled boxes or areas for different items; a box of bags and a row of buggies. Could you adapt a children's shopping trolley to help transport items to the different storage areas?

8. Arrange a rota for the attendants with somewhere to take their tea breaks.

9. Travellers can retrieve their luggage by showing attendants their receipts at the window. Now the attendants will find out how efficient their system of storage really is! Encourage them to make improvements or modifications if necessary.

More little ideas:

▶ Involve the children in making a mock X-ray scanning machine to check that the contents of the bags are safe. You could cut away a big cardboard box to make a tunnel shape to pass the bags through. Consider representing the contents of the bags with pictures, perhaps cut from clothing catalogues, stuck onto the sides of the box. What else could be inside the bags?

▶ Think about packing. Provide the children with a mixed collection of clothes and other props to sort and pack for different weather conditions or destinations.

▶ Set up a shop nearby selling luggage and travel accessories.

▶ A left luggage point would work well as a second role play area alongside a station (see 'On the right Track' page 33).

Need a Car?

Add a new twist to your outside play with ride on toys by introducing a car hire service.

Starting points:

▶ Explore with the children the idea of hiring something, perhaps by relating it to their experience of borrowing and returning a library book or taking their learning journeys home and bringing them back.

▶ Try to arrange a visit to a car hire or car wash or invite a member of staff to come and talk to the children about their job.

▶ Children might have experienced an automatic car wash or jet wash.

▶ Their families might have hired cars on holidays or when a family car has been out of use. Talk through ideas with the children and together plan your role play area.

Set up the role play window:

1. Set up the role play window on a table. Include a cash till and means of paying, paper and mark making equipment.

2. Make additional phones available so that customers can reserve cars by phone. Will there be a different charge for bikes and cars?

3. Number the cars with labels either tied on or fixed with sticky tape. Park them in "bays" numbered with chalk. Make and number sets of keys for them. (Either use old keys or laminated images of keys).

4. On arrival, customers can go to the window, show their driving licence (see photocopiable driving licence, page 74) and be told which number car they have hired. Helpful staff can be available to guide them to it.

5. On return cars will need a thorough wash before hiring to the next customer. Staff training might involve talking about the sequence of activities involved in washing a car: washing with soapy water, rinsing, drying and polishing. Provide buckets and sponges, aprons, old towels and pieces of tubing/vacuum nozzles – any junk you can find – but risk assess first. The cars will need to be cleaned inside too. Cars will then need to be returned to the appropriate numbered bay.

More little ideas:

▶ Make an automatic car wash: Set up two tables with a corridor between for vehicles to drive through. Attach a feather duster to the front leg of each table. Make a stop/go traffic light from a piece of card with a red circle on one side and a green on the other. Attendants could write a code number that will start the automatic car wash. Customers could enter this number on the role play window key pad.

▶ Together with the children, devise a questionnaire for customers. Are they happy with the service and the cleanliness of the vehicles? Would they use your company again? Completed questionnaires could be handed in at the role play window.

▶ Management could encourage and reward staff with a 'Car Washer of the Day' award.

▶ Combine this with bus role play (see 'The Wheels on the Bus' page 25) or garage role play (see 'Fill up with Fuel' page 29).

▶ Depending on children's experiences this activity can easily be adapted to be a boat hire. Add some cardboard oars and a megaphone for "Come in Number 5!"

Have a nice stay!

Turn your home area into holiday accommodation with reception desk.

Starting points:

▶ Draw on the children's own experiences of holidays and use this to help plan your role play together. Some might have stayed in hotels or travel inns, some at holiday camps or on caravan sites; settings at which they will have experienced "checking in".

▶ Talk about what happened at the reception desk: What did the receptionist say and do? What happened to their luggage? What was their key like and how did it work?

▶ Talk about the accommodation and resort: What was different from home? What did they like and dislike about it?

Set up the role play window:

1. Use the role play window as Reception. Include mark-making equipment and make simple pictorial forms for checking in and paying bills. Number cards to be electronic keys, or tie numbered labels to more conventional keys.

2. Make a set of pigeon holes from shoe boxes with numbers corresponding to keys and room numbers. Use them for incoming mail and messages and to keep the corresponding accommodation keys in. Alternatively make a board with numbered hooks or pockets.

3. Include a keyboard, a cash till and means of paying. Phones can be used to take bookings and to provide room service. Make sure trays, cups, plates and play food are to hand if this service is to be included. Alternatively incorporate your snack time into the play and use real food.

4. Guests may need to show passports, (see photocopiable page 73).

5. Accommodation will depend on your existing facilities: a home corner can be subdivided with a screen to make two rooms; pop up tents or giant boxes could serve as additional rooms or caravans. Number each room to correspond with its key.

6. Talk about how you can make guests as comfortable as possible so that they return for another visit. Perhaps you can provide a welcome tray with cups and saucers and a toy kettle or some of the freebie shower caps etc. from real hotels. Make sure none of these present a health hazard and supervise according to any risk assessment.

More little ideas:

▶ Who will maintain the accommodation? Provide cleaning equipment/ trolleys. Together make door hanging signs for guests to use according to whether they want their rooms made up, or do not wish to be disturbed.

▶ Perhaps some redecoration will be needed from time to time. Provide large paintbrushes, tubs with handles and sheets to cover furniture.

▶ Combine the role play area with a restaurant for guests. Combine with a car park (see 'Park your Car' page 27) and note the vehicle number on check in. Add some holiday attractions (see 'Happy Holidays!' and 'More Happy Holidays!' pages 43 and 45).

▶ Ask for visitor feedback. Do guests have any suggestions for improving the service? Provide a Visitors' Book or suggestion cards for guests to fill in. These could be posted in the window.

Happy Holidays!

Use children's own holiday experiences as the inspiration for your window play.

Starting points:

► Talk to the children about their favourite holiday experiences or days out.

► Many tourist attractions involve a window for selling tickets and giving information. The activities and ideas outlined here could be adapted according to children's own holiday memories.

► Involve parents in providing photographs and adding to children's holiday stories.

► Collect relevant leaflets and maps to share with the children.

► Look online for information and images of places children have visited.

Theme Park
If children are excited by visits to theme parks, why not create one in your setting.

Set up the role play window: ———————————

1. Use the role play window to sell tickets and give out maps or information leaflets made by the children. Include a cash till and some means to pay.

2. If you already have permanent play equipment in place you could rename it as rides; the slide might become a log flume, a climbing frame might become a crazy house or a roundabout a waltzer. You might transform other play equipment; trikes might become quad bikes, or pedal cars could be numbered to make dodgems. Talk to the children about their favourite rides and think about how you could adapt your own play equipment accordingly.

3. Organise a queue for tickets at the window using cones. Dress up a performer to entertain the queue. Have a collector ready to take tickets from the 'guests' before they go to play.

4. For ideas about incorporating maps in this play see 'The Little Book of Maps and Plans'.

Fairground
Have children been to the fair on a seaside holiday? Replicate all the fun of the fair in your setting.

Set up the role play window: ———————————

1. Use the role play window to issue wrist bands made of strips of coloured card for unlimited play. If these are to be 'sold' you will need a cash till and some means to pay.

2. Set up any games you may already have such as skittles, quoits and beanbag games. Number the skittles and quoits to encourage number recognition through play.

3. Involve the children in designing and making their own throwing games; maybe aiming beanbags at numbered bins or buckets, or throwing rings from a quoits set over various small world toys. Can the children think of any good names for their new games?

4. Make your own 'Hook a Duck' type game, perhaps using fishing nets to catch ducks floating in a paddling pool.

5. Think about adding some small scale theme park type attractions such as pedal car dodgems or trike quad bikes.

More Happy Holidays!

More window ideas to create a holiday atmosphere without leaving your setting.

Model Village

Have any of the children visited a model village? Use their memories to help build one together.

Set up the role play window:

► Provide a cash till and use the role play window to sell tickets to visit the model village.

► Think about the shape and purpose of different kinds of buildings. The children might make a replica of their own village or high street or plan and create their own town.

► Use construction kits or junk materials to make the buildings according to children's interests. Encourage the children to experiment with different building and fixing techniques. Arrange the buildings on a road mat or involve the children in drawing roads on big sheets of paper. Add small world play figures and vehicles.

► Consider making a route for visitors around the model village. Will the children need to make arrows or signs to encourage a one way system?

► Take photos of the village to be made into a souvenir guide for families to see.

▶ Think about designing a model village map or some 'Can you find...?' pictorial quiz sheets to be attached to clipboards and given out at the window. Don't forget to provide pencils.

Mini Golf Course
If children have had fun playing mini golf, plan and set up your own mini golf course together.

Set up the role play window:

1. The role play window could be used for the distribution and collection of golf clubs and balls. Decide together if golfers will 'pay' for each round at the window. If so, add a cash till and some means to pay. Think about providing storage for the clubs and balls alongside the window.

2. Children's mini golf sets with numbered holes are commercially available, but you can also make 'holes' from junk materials, for example cut tunnel shaped holes at either end of an upturned shoe box. You will need about six holes to start with.

3. Talk about setting up the course with the holes in numerical order. Encourage the children to think about position and spacing. Try the course out and rearrange the holes if necessary.

4. Design some golf score cards to be given out at the window. Make simple sheets with a clip art golf logo and a number line at the top to be attached to a clipboard for children to record their scores in their own way. Provide some pencils or pens.

5. For ideas about incorporating maps in this play see 'The Little Book of Maps and Plans'.

More little ideas:
▶ According to children's experiences, use your role play window to sell tickets and provide information and maps for city bus tours, boat trips or steam train rides. Provide microphones for commentators and use the ideas in 'The Wheels on the Bus' page 25 and 'On the right Track' page 33 to develop and enhance children's play.

▶ A café with play food or real food would work well alongside any of these tourist attractions.

▶ Add some holiday accommodation as a second role play situation (see 'Have a nice stay!' page 41).

Ice, ice baby!

Make your own ice cream van. As with all activities involving food, ensure children with allergies are identified and catered for, risk assess the activity thoroughly and use the opportunity to reinforce hand hygiene.

Starting points:

▶ Arrange for an ice cream van to visit, or visit an event where an ice cream van is set up

▶ Talk about the children's experiences of ice cream vans. What was for sale and what were their favourite things to buy? You might talk about ice lollies, cones, ninety nines.

▶ Discuss favourite flavours. Which flavours go together well?

▶ Has anyone ever made ice cream or lollies?

▶ Talk about safety around the van, especially about crossing roads. Involve the children in role plays to illustrate the dangers of running towards or away from the van and to make them aware of other vehicles that might be nearby.

▶ Talk about healthy choices. Discuss what kinds of food are good for us and which foods should be eaten in moderation, as a treat.

Set up the role play window:

1. Place the window on a table so that ice cream can be sold through it. You could stick wheels to the table legs for added authenticity: cut circles of card or use paper plates. If you can source an old trolley to put it on, a mobile window could visit and stop at different parts of your setting.

2. Include a cash box and means of paying. Add a phone handset to call for more stock. Provide notebooks for taking orders and calculators for totting up.

3. Provide hats, aprons and name labels for staff.

4. Think of a name for your ice cream company and make a label for the window.

5. A xylophone, megaphone or portable music player can be useful to announce the vans arrival. If you have a music recorder, have fun making up and recording jingles.

6. Make your stock.

The Real Thing...

A fun activity is to make real ice lollies with the children. This also provides opportunities for the children to observe changes; water becoming ice in the freezing process then melting as it becomes warm.

▶ Lolly moulds and sticks are inexpensive to buy. Commercially produced lolly makers are available and produce lollies in minutes if you have access to a freezer compartment. Ask around to see if you can borrow one from families or friends. There is a wealth of opportunity for making exciting flavours with different juices or milkshakes, and for embedding various fruits.

▶ Use the opportunity to talk again about healthy choices, to discuss colour, transparency and opaqueness and involve the children fully in the design and manufacture.

▶ Think up names for your lollies together, such as "Strawberry Surprise" or "Raspberry Rocket".

▶ As a snack time treat, provide tubs of ice cream, sauces, sprinkles and cut up fruits together. Design, make and name exotic fruity ice cream sundaes. Take photos for display.

Let's Pretend.....

There are many ways to make pretend stock; anything that comes in a variety of colours will capture children's imagination:

▶ Make cones from circles of stiff paper. Cut a slit from one edge to the middle, pull to overlap an edge and form a cone shape, then secure with tape.

▶ Provide small tubs and plastic spoons or plastic sundae glasses.

▶ Provide a variety of collage materials to make the ice creams; cotton wool, shredded paper, glitter for sprinkles, and wool for sauces. Ask the children for ideas.

▶ Use pegs as sticks and provide brightly coloured card to make the lolly tops.

▶ Outside, sand works well as a filling and sticks serve well as chocolate flakes!

More little ideas:

▶ Encourage the children to design in 2D, gluing on layers to make an ice cream collage. Stick these to a large board to stand outside the van and add prices.

▶ Can you design a junk model machine to dispense pretend ice cream?

▶ Think up snappy rhyming straplines to promote your ice creams; "Forget the rest, our ice creams are the best!" or "Buy a lolly from Mrs Jolly!"

▶ Combine with other role play scenarios. (See ideas in 'Happy Holidays!' and 'More Happy Holidays!' pages 43-45).

Take a walk on the Wild Side

Create a wildlife park in your setting and include the children's favourite animals

Starting points:

▶ This is an ideal role play if you can organise a visit to a local wildlife park or smaller animal park. Take plenty of photos.

▶ Draw on the children's experiences, share photos, books, souvenirs and stories.

▶ Some parks and zoos will bring animals to your setting for close encounters. Find out from the handlers how to look after the animals.

Set up the role play window: ————————

1. Include tickets, cash till and means of paying.

2. Divide your area into smaller enclosures using chalk, masking tape or barriers.

3. Animals could be cuddly toys or made by the children e.g. papier mache/junk. Alternatively make animal masks for living, moving animals! Your park might have a wide range of animals or specialise, for example, in birds or monkeys.

4. Keepers will need to feed, care for and clean out the animals' shelters. Provide mops, buckets, brushes, labelled caps, protective clothing, clipboards and pens. Keepers might need to mark when the animals have been fed and whether they are looking healthy. Use old shirts to make keepers' uniforms with stickers for name badges. Keepers will also need walkie talkies or mobile phones (toys or old phones no longer in use).

5. Fill junk containers with animal feed; use small items like conkers, acorns or other natural materials.

6. Find out what different animals like to eat and include it on a pictorial sign beside the enclosure. Other information that could be displayed pictorially might be whether the animals live in water, on land or in the air and whether they prefer hot or cold conditions.

7. Together make a large map of the park, reduce and photocopy it to make a leaflet for guests on their way in. Place it next to the window.

8. Encourage guests to take photos with real or toy digital cameras. These can be displayed or made into a souvenir album later. Guests might also have toy binoculars.

9. If little train rides are on offer you could also sell tickets for these. A stretchy piece of elastic made from old tights tied together will allow the train driver and passengers to be linked and travel round the park but ensure children are supervised and explain safety rules to them. Add the route of your train to your map.

10. Guests could go on an animal trail, ticking off animals as they see them. You could make a tick sheet showing pictures (photos or children's own) of animals in your park. Photocopy and place by the role play window. Give them out to visitors as they enter. You could offer a small prize to those who complete them (e.g. children could make book marks to give away).

More little ideas:

▶ Keepers or other animal experts can give talks about the animals and allow guests to have close encounters. Arrange chairs for an instant amphitheatre and add whiteboard/paper/pens/information books/pictures/posters.

▶ Add a souvenir shop. Use your small world animals as toys to sell and collect ideas from the children as to what else should be on sale.

▶ Take the opportunity to talk about looking after animals properly, size of enclosures and how such parks can help endangered species.

▶ Link the safari park to other role play areas. Include a café/restaurant and a car park (see 'Park your Car' page 27). Vehicles that visit might have a decorated sticker to help advertise the park to other children. Some animals might need to see the vet (see 'Visit to the Vet' page 53).

Visit to the Vet

Use role play to share and build on children's experiences of caring for their pets.

Starting points:

▶ Encourage children to talk about their own experiences and knowledge about keeping a pet; this might be their own pet or a pet belonging to another family member, neighbour or friend. Take the opportunity to learn about what pets need to be happy and healthy and the responsibilities of being a pet owner. Children will enjoy being the experts!

▶ Think carefully about the possibility of letting the children experience being with an animal. Would a member of staff be able to bring a pet in? Do remember that if owners bring their pets into your setting you will need to risk assess and get parental permissions first.

▶ Have any of the children or staff visited the vet's with their pets? Listen to their stories.

▶ Talk about what a vet does: caring for pets, wild animals, farm animals and animals kept in zoos or wildlife parks. There are lots of children's stories, non- fiction books, computer programs and television series about the subject. Have the children watched programmes about an animal hospital? Maybe you can arrange for a vet to come and talk to the children.

Set up the role play window:

1. The role play window will act as the Reception area within the Vet's Waiting Room.

2. The vet's receptionist or office manager can sit at the window and issue appointment slips or numbered cards to pet owners so that the vet can see them in order. Appointments might also be made by phone. A dummy computer with keyboard would allow staff to check availability of appointments. Add a cash till for payment of bills.

3. Begin by making a collection of soft toy pets to take to the vets. (School fairs and charity shops are a good source or ask for donations.) Add toy animal carriers, a doctor's set for the vet, long and short bandages and sticky tape to fix them. Lolly sticks make good splints.

4. A few chairs, some non-fiction books about animals on a table and a clock will serve as a Waiting Room. Ask the children to bring in photographs of family or neighbours' pets. Add magazine pictures and clip art and encourage children to use these images to make their own posters, leaflets or booklets for the waiting room.

5. The vet will need an examining table and trays or boxes for the instruments and bandages. A nurse might assist the vet or take notes. Provide a clipboard and blank index cards.

6. The receptionist can issue bills after each appointment. Does the owner need to come back for another appointment next week?

More little ideas:

▶ Photograph the soft toy animals and make named record cards for the vet or nurse to refer to and update.

▶ Set up a counter selling pet accessories such as balls, bowls and combs. Make pet food labels to stick on your play food tins.

▶ Make additional animal carriers or beds from cardboard boxes and junk materials. Involve the children in thinking about shape and size. Will the dog fit in the bed?

▶ Use your props to make an Animal Rescue Centre or Pet Shop.

▶ Use non-fiction books and the internet to find out more about animals according to children's interests.

Stadium for Sports Stars

Nurture a love of sport in your setting.

Starting points:

▶ Talk to the children about their experience of sport. What sports do they enjoy? Does anyone go to football training or swimming lessons? Who likes running? Some of the children might support a particular team or have experience of watching a sporting event. Ask parents, carers and adults in your setting about their involvement in sport.

▶ Think about developing the activity play already popular in your setting. New sports are introduced to the Olympics at every Games. Why shouldn't mini golf, beanbag throwing or walking on balance boards become an international sport?

▶ Alternatively, a local team or stadium might be the focus of your play. If possible, start with a visit, or look at images of the stadium online. Look at the facilities for sportspeople and spectators and how the space is organised. Find out more about the relevant sport.

▶ A major sporting event might be imminent, like the Olympics, the Commonwealth Games or the World Cup. Perhaps you could host one of these events in your sports stadium.

▶ Now decide together what sports will take place in your own sports stadium.

Set up the role play window:

1. The role play window will act as the ticket booth. Children might be team members, spectators, officials or announcers.

2. Think about building an inspiring grand entrance to the stadium with some giant building blocks or boxes. Add an entrance banner or poster.

3. Involve the children in making tickets for spectators and passes for team members and announcers; these could be checked by officials at the window. Look at examples of logos from real sporting events online and help the children to design, scan and print their own logo to be used on posters, signs and sticker badges.

4. For the team members, number plain T-shirts or vests with fabric pens or put low tack numbered stickers on children's own clothes. In athletics events, runners could match these numbers to numbered lanes.

5. Mark out the playing area using chalk, ribbon or masking tape. Adapt and simplify conventional markings according to the size and shape of your area. In an athletics stadium you might have numbered lanes for running, two arcs marked out for throwing; one to stand inside and one to throw at, and a circuit around the outside for speed walking. Jumpers would need safety mats. Unless you have a very big space, officials would be well advised to have running, throwing and jumping events on different days! In a football stadium there might be a centre circle and chalked marks for the goals. Pop-up goals would be a luxury! Put a row of chairs for spectators in a safe place and risk assess the area and equipment before play.

6. Present the event itself as a chance to 'have a go' at your chosen sport. Young children can find competition difficult so don't look for winners but be inclusive, awarding certificates and medals to everyone and congratulating them for taking part. (Medals are available as party bag toys, or make your own.)

7. Enhance the role of spectators by providing toy cameras, binoculars and video cameras if you have them. Supporters might wear team scarves or hold up home – made banners or flags. Compose some appropriate chants and songs together.

8. Provide microphones for announcers. Adults could model naming the team and commentating and then children could take over.

9. Don't forget to film the event and take photographs which might be made into a souvenir programme for families to see.

More little ideas:

▶ Is there an international element to your event? If so, some children in your setting might have family links with other countries taking part and others might have been on holiday abroad. This might lead to further investigation with maps. (See 'The Little Book of Maps and Plans').

▶ Adapt some of the ideas in this activity to make a Sports Centre with the emphasis on participation. Include some musical exercise classes, football training sessions, trampolining, basketball and tennis with foam balls. Risk assess the area and equipment. Staff at the role play window could issue and check leisure passes, give directions and provide information about sessions and classes.

Fancy Dress Fun

Open a fancy dress hire shop using your dressing up clothes.

Starting points:

▶ Involve a group of children who love to dress up. Talk to them about their favourite outfits and where they like to wear them. Have any of the children ever been to a fancy dress party before?

▶ Introduce the idea of organising a fancy dress party or parade in your setting. These make good fundraisers as well as being a focus for dressing up. Children with an interest in music could choose the songs for the parade or play musical instruments in a band.

▶ Encouraging children to plan and play their own pretend parties in the home area also gives dressing up a purpose. Add party tableware, a play birthday cake and a birthday banner. Provide resources for making and writing greetings cards and invitations.

▶ Explain how the hire shop might work. Customers pay a fee to borrow an outfit from the shop for a special occasion. They promise to take care of the clothes and return them so that they can be hired by someone else. (Link to ideas about borrowing and returning in 'Borrow a Book' page 23 and 'Need a Car?' page 39).

Set up the role play window:

1. The role play window will be the focus of the fancy dress hire shop. The shop owner can sit behind it to greet and direct visitors, take orders by phone and order stock on the 'computer'.

2. The owner will need a helpful assistant on the shop floor to advise customers. Initially adults may need to help by modelling the language; "Do you need a hat with that?", "You look great!" "Please bring the clothes back in good condition next week."

3. Before play begins, focus on your collection of dressing up clothes. Revitalise your stock by washing, mending and customising existing clothes. Visit charity shops and ask for donations and help from parents and carers who can sew!

4. Involve the children in sorting and presenting the clothes for 'customers', for example you might have superhero costumes at one end of the clothes rail and animal costumes at the other. Try to avoid gender stereotyping. Sort accessories into labelled boxes such as 'hats' and 'bags'.

5. Make masks to hire. A face shape or a paper plate with a lolly stick handle taped to the base makes a safe mask for young children.

6. Use a screen to make a changing room. Add a sign and a full length mirror.

7. Customers should return to the window to pay for the hire of their outfits. Provide a cash till and a pad for the play writing of receipts.

8. Sell blank party invitations at the window for home area party play.

9. At the end of the session customers can return their outfits at the role play window. The owner and assistant will need to tidy up and check that everything has been returned before closing.

More little ideas:

▶ Take photographs of children wearing the costumes and use these to make a numbered catalogue of outfits. Include the children in taking the photographs and in writing and ordering the numbers. Leave the catalogue by the role play window for reference.

▶ Encourage children to create their own fancy dress designs using a variety of media including drawings, collages and paintings. Display these designs in the role play area around the window.

▶ Link the fancy dress hire shop to your theme park. (See ideas for creating a theme park in 'The Little Book of Maps and Plans' or develop and extend the activities in 'Fairground', 'Happy Holidays!' page 44).

▶ Use your fancy dress hire shop to help celebrate the Jewish festival of Purim. At Purim, Jewish families join parades wearing fancy dress as part of their celebrations. Take the opportunity to learn more about this festival.

Create an Art Gallery

Create an Art Gallery to display and provide an audience for children's work.

Starting points:

- ▶ Are you lucky enough to be able to visit an art gallery or local exhibition of art work with the children?
- ▶ Have any of the children or adults visited an art gallery before? Talk about children's impressions of what a gallery might be like and what might happen there.
- ▶ Use the internet to find images of galleries, outside and inside.
- ▶ Contact an art class and see if you can arrange a visit from an artist to show and talk about their work and how it is displayed.
- ▶ Explore the idea of finding an audience. Who would the children like to show their pictures to?

Set up the role play window:

1. The role play window will form the entrance to your gallery. Use it to collect invitations, give out response cards and sell postcards (see below). Gallery staff might need a phone, writing materials and a cash till.

2. Begin by encouraging the children to create works of art for the gallery. Include paintings, drawings and collages. Don't forget to ask them to name or sign their work.

3. Include the children in thinking about the wording and design of invitations, perhaps to parents and carers, asking them to visit the gallery and view the pictures.

4. Involve the children in designing frames for their pictures, choosing colours for mounting them, and then decorating the borders. Provide coloured foil, plastic gems, buttons, shells, small stickers etc.

5. Set up your gallery together. Display the pictures on walls and mobile boards if you have them. Put a number beside each picture. Print children's titles and thoughts about their pictures underneath. Older children will be able to record these captions themselves. Add some chairs for viewing the pictures.

6. Provide blank postcards for children to draw on. These could be laminated and sold at the window, or the children could set up a gallery shop and café alongside the window.

7. Open your gallery. Welcome visitors and model talk which encourages all the children to look at, talk about and value each other's pictures.

More little ideas:

▶ Make a record of the exhibition with a catalogue showing photographs of each picture. Include names of artists, numbers, titles and captions.

▶ For 'artists in residence', relocate your Creative Area within the gallery, providing easels and a large table with a variety of art materials.

▶ Make a Sculpture Gallery displaying models made of junk, clay or dough.

▶ Use similar ideas to set up a Museum displaying collections according to children's interests, for example dinosaurs or model cars.

Click and Collect

Set up a Collection Point for online shopping.

Starting points:

▶ Talk about children's experience of different kinds of shopping: supermarket shopping, city centre shopping, corner shops, out of town retail parks and so on. Encourage children to share their shopping stories.

▶ Have any children had experience of choosing toys, clothing or even food online and collecting them from a store?

▶ Move your laptop into the Home area to enrich children's role play or use a dummy computer screen and keyboard.

Set up the role play window:

Set up two role play areas; one in the Home area with pretend computer facilities for ordering online, and another Collection Point area based around the role play window for picking up shopping ordered at 'home'.

Home area:

1. Talk about how and where computers are used in children's homes. Will they need a quiet area, a desk or just a sofa and a laptop cushion?

2. Provide an old PC or laptop or involve the children in making a junk model laptop. You might use two sides of a cardboard box with the edge representing the hinge between screen and keyboard. Paint it black and stick on a thin piece of black card for the screen. Images of computer keyboards are available online and one of these could be printed out, laminated and stuck on.

3. Make a sheet to stick onto the dummy computer screen with a grid for six to eight numbered items, maybe toys, clothes or food items, depending on children's experience of online shopping. Add small photos of the items or use pictures cut from catalogues. You could produce a few of these sheets for variety or to extend play.

4. Make your own credit cards as a means to pay; print children's names, add a card number and a space for children to sign. Laminate the cards to make them sturdy.

5. However impressive your cardboard computer might look, it will be unable to print out an email! As a substitute, children will need to complete simple order forms themselves. These forms could be kept and completed in the Home area. According to the ability of the children, the order forms might have pictures of the items for children to circle, numbers of the items for children to circle or boxes for children to write their own numbers. Older children might be able to copy their credit card numbers onto the form too. This would help them to understand that payment is made before collection.

Collection Point:

1. Customers will travel from the home area to the role play window collection point, hand their order forms in and collect their chosen items. Staff might ask for identification (see photocopiable passport and driving licence pages 73 and 74).

2. Now think about how your stock is going to be organised. Arrange the items for collection on a table alongside the window and number them to correspond with the numbers on the computer screen and order forms. You will need additional staff at the table to retrieve the objects that have been ordered.

3. Alternatively, it might be more realistic to have items stored out of sight in a screened off back area. Do the children have any ideas about how window staff might communicate with the stockroom workers? Think about adding phones, microphones, a junk box intercom or another member of staff to deliver order forms by hand.

4. Add some seats for customers waiting to be served. Enjoy your shopping!

More little ideas:

▶ Encourage customer feedback. Produce some sheets with pictures of each item and a row of stars for children to colour in.

▶ Have a Home Delivery service with ride-on vehicles.

▶ Depending on the seller, Collection Points can be found in large stores, corner shops and even petrol stations. Ask children and families where online shopping is collected in your area and think about adding one of these role play scenarios to your own Collection Point.

▶ Bring more shopping fun into the Home area with a selection of catalogues, or encourage children to make their own.

To boldly go...

Buy a ticket to the moon.

Starting points:

▶ Children's interest in Space might come from television, film, favourite stories or small world play. Show children images of space travel, moon landings and astronauts online.

▶ There are some delightful Space stories to expand children's imaginations such as:

  ▷ 'Man in the Moon' by Simon Bartram

  ▷ 'Whatever Next' by Jill Murphy

  ▷ 'QPootle5' by Nick Butterworth

In 'Man in the Moon', Bob, is a tour guide on the moon and a site manager; we see him hoovering around the craters! The juxtaposition of the fantasy and excitement of his job with everyday routines would help children to use both their own experiences and their imaginations in this play.

▶ Involve families in helping children to look at the sky on a clear night. What differences can they see between night and day? Can they see any stars? What shape is the moon? Winter nights, when it gets dark early, are a good time for this activity!

Set up the role play window:

1. Imagine that the role play window is a futuristic ticket and information office for space flights. This role play would work particularly well outside!

2. Talk about possible destinations for the space flights. Will you fly to the moon or cruise around the stars? Can the children name any planets? Will space tourists be required to show their passports at the window before travelling? (See photocopiable passport page 73).

3. Involve the children in making flight tickets and rocket seat reservation cards for space tourists. Number the reservation cards to correspond with the number of seats on the rocket. Use self-adhesive stars or little stickers with a space theme for decoration. Add a cash till behind the window and some means to pay.

4. Children with an interest in space might enjoy making simple information leaflets about various planets. Help them to find and print clip art illustrations and provide some non-fiction books about space for reference.

5. Use a table alongside the window to set up a souvenir stand like Bob's in 'Man on the Moon'. Sell your small world space toys as souvenir models and encourage the children to draw space pictures on blank postcards. Make space flags by taping a triangle or rectangle of paper onto a thin drinking straw. Decorate with pictures of the planets; drawn or clip art.

6. Display children's paintings with a space or rocket theme around the window. Add a poster of the solar system if you have one.

7. Build a rocket! The story 'Whatever Next' shows how even the simplest materials can be combined with children's imagination to make a spaceship! Provide junk materials, boxes, big building bricks and plenty of silver foil. Suggest adding a control panel and some numbered seats.

8. Adapt your outdoor clothing to look like space suits by adding stickers with space logos or flags. For added authenticity paint two cereal boxes and join at the top with two shoulder straps, add two plastic bottles as oxygen tanks with some bits of hose or plastic tubing; attach with strips of silver duct tape. Wear wellies for space walking.

9. Check the engines before counting backwards for lift off. The pilot might need a microphone for in flight information.

10. Touchdown! Take ideas from the children about how you might represent another planet in part of your outside area; think about draping fabric or arranging rocks and other natural materials in unusual ways. Add some atmospheric music and a box of musical instruments. Risk assess your alien landscape before play.

11. Experiment with different ways of moving in space. Look at videos of astronauts floating weightless online for ideas.

More little ideas:

▶ Serve space snacks on board: Make star shaped biscuits and serve melon slices shaped like crescent moons. Kiwi slices look like planets too.

▶ Add a Magazine Kiosk (see 'Read all about it!' page 17). In 'Man on the Moon' Bob reads his paper and does the crossword on his way to the moon.

▶ In the story 'QPootle5' the space rocket breaks down. Add a rocket garage with appropriate spare parts.

Make a busy School Office

Use role play to support children making the transition to school.

Starting points:

▶ School office play would interest children transferring from a nursery or pre-school setting to 'big' school. Children can be both excited and apprehensive about this change, and this role play would answer their questions and prompt further discussion. It could also be used in the early weeks at school. In both situations school office role play would help to build confidence and familiarity with school routines, geography and personnel.

▶ Visit the school office as part of a tour of the school. Meet the office staff, learn their names and encourage children to ask questions about what happens in the office. What do they use the computer for? What do people phone up about? Why do children, parents and school staff come to the office?

▶ Talk about office staff as part of the 'family' of people who will help children in their new school, including teachers, lunchtime assistants, classroom assistants, learning assistants and older children.

Set up the role play window:

1. Make the role play window the hub of your office. Add desks and chairs, an extra phone and plenty of stationery for writing messages and notices. A whiteboard and pen would be useful for reminders.

2. Involve the children in using clip art to make some school headed notepaper. Add envelopes and put them in a tray or box by the role play window. Suggest composing play letters to parents about school trips, dinner money and the naming of uniform. Think back to your office visit for ideas.

3. Add other office accessories such as a variety of pens and pencils organised in a holder, paper clips, sticky notes and a diary.

4. Explain that office staff need to know which children are in school. Talk about registration and have a children's signing in and out book on a table in front of the role play window for children coming in late or leaving early. Support children in writing their own names in the book as part of their play.

5. Include a wall planner or calendar and a clock. Display a list of times for breaks and lunch.

6. Use the role play window to 'sell' items of school uniform, (ask for donations) and empty water bottles. You will need a cash box.

7. Make a 'stock room' with paper, folders, exercise books, pencils and crayons neatly stacked.

More little ideas:

▶ Combine the office area with playing school. Mimic the school day: start with news and notices and have a bell for a 15 minute play outside. Encourage the children to take turns at being the teacher, classroom assistant and school children. Include familiar play activities such as story time, singing, counting and rhyming games. Focus on similarities in routines between settings as well as differences.

▶ Talk about the role of the office in counting children's meals. Look at some sample menus for school dinners. What meal would you choose? Draw your packed lunch inside a lunchbox shape.

▶ Make a simple map or plan of the school together to show where the office is situated.

▶ Make a desk tidy with junk materials.

Everyday Window Play

Incorporate window play in everyday routines in your setting.

Starting points:

▶ Introduce photos of the daily activities that all children take part in. These might include registration, snack time, circle time and home time as well as all kinds of indoor and outdoor play. Talk about and sequence the activities; do the children have any favourites? Talk about likes and dislikes and use children's ideas to inform your future planning.

▶ Can the children see any opportunities for using the role play window in everyday routines? Could you enliven your routines by engaging children in a more playful way?

▶ The activities below might provide some ideas and fun learning opportunities which could be adapted for your own setting and procedures.

Self-Registration
Use the role play window in self- registration.

1. Make name cards with a colour code or picture symbol for each Key group.
2. Arrange the name cards in Key groups on a table alongside the role play window.

3. To register, children might find their own name card and pass it to children acting as 'staff' or 'helpers' behind the window. Adults could model a friendly greeting!

4. Children behind the window could then use their mathematical skills to sort the name cards back into Key groups and count them to find the total number of children present.

Outdoor Play Staffed Cloakroom
Give out and collect in protective clothing for outdoor play using the role play window.

1. Involve the children in sorting your outdoor clothing, such as waterproofs and sun hats, into boxes, or use clothes rails if you have them.

2. Create themed decorations for your cloakroom, for example representations of clothing, weather and seasons.

3. Children wanting to play outside could ask for appropriate clothing at the window and attendants could then pass clothes across a table next to the window. Adults might need to model and encourage the kind of language used in these transactions: "Can I have a coat, please." "Yes, Joseph. Do you need wellies too?"

4. At the end of the session, attendants can collect the items and count them before tidying up.

Snack Kiosk
Help deliver snack time with the role play window.

1. Think about using the role play window as a food kiosk to involve children in preparing and giving out simple snacks such as fresh fruit or raw vegetables and drinks such as bottled water.

2. Alternatively, children behind the window might organise and give out plates, bowls, spoons and cups while food might be presented on tables alongside the window for children to serve themselves.

3. Consider using your name cards and the role play window to monitor which children have had snack. (See Self-Registration).

More little ideas:
▶ Do you have a box full of unclaimed items that nobody is interested in? Label the role play window 'Lost Property' and involve the children in the puzzle of identifying and returning items themselves.

▶ Involve children in giving out letters at home time through the role play window, under adult supervision!

Appendix

Passport

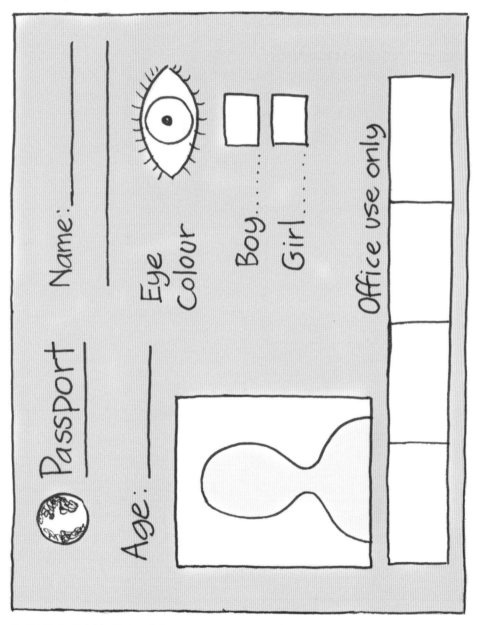

Driving Licence

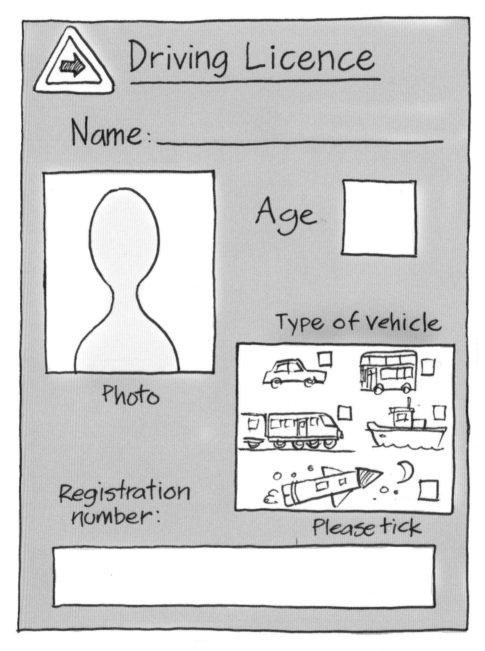

If you have found this book useful you might also like...

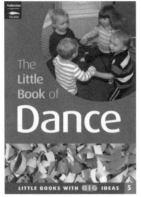

LB Dance
ISBN 978-1-9041-8774-5

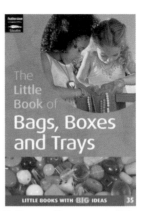

LB Bags, Boxes and Trays
ISBN 978-1-9050-1909-0

LB Clothes and Fabrics
ISBN 978-1-9050-1969-4

LB Sound Ideas
ISBN 978-1-9050-1955-7

All available from

www.bloomsbury.com/featherstone

LB Making Poetry
ISBN 978-1-4081-1250-2

LB Christmas
ISBN 978-1-9022-3364-2

LB Discovery Bottles
ISBN 978-1-9060-2971-5

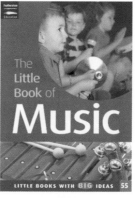

LB Music
ISBN 978-1-9041-8754-7

All available from
www.bloomsbury.com/featherstone

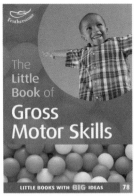

LB Gross Motor Skills
ISBN 978-1-4081-5545-5

LB Growing Things
ISBN 978-1-9041-8768-4

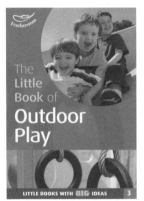

LB Outdoor Play
ISBN 978-1-9022-3374-1

LB Games with Sounds
ISBN 978-1-9060-2911-1

All available from

www.bloomsbury.com/featherstone

The Little Books Club

There is always something in Little Books to help and inspire you.
Packed full of lovely ideas, Little Books meet the need for exciting and
practical activities that are fun to do, address the Early Learning Goals
and can be followed in most settings. Everyone is a winner!

We publish 5 new Little Books a year. Little Books Club members receive
each of these 5 books as soon as they are published for a reduced price.
The subscription cost is £29.99 – a one off payment that buys
the 5 new books for £4.99 instead of £8.99 each.

In addition to this, Little Books Club Members receive:
· Free postage and packing on anything ordered from the
  Featherstone catalogue
· A 15% discount voucher upon joining which can be used to buy any
  number of books from the Featherstone catalogue
· Members price of £4.99 on any additional Little Book purchased
· A regular, free newsletter featuring club news, free activity ideas and
  aspects of Early Years curriculum and practice from experts in the
  industry
· All new Little Books on approval - return in good condition within 30
  days and we'll refund the cost to your club account

Call 020 7758 0200 or email: littlebooks@bloomsbury.com for
an enrolment pack. Or download an application form from our website:
www.bloomsbury.com/featherstone

The Little Books series consists of:

All Through the Year

Bags, Boxes & Trays

Big Projects

Bricks and Boxes

Celebrations

Christmas

Circle Time

Clay and Malleable
Materials

Clothes and Fabrics

Colour, Shape and Number

Cooking from Stories

Cooking Together

Counting

Dance

Dance, with music CD

Discovery Bottles

Dough

Drama from Stories

50

Explorations

Fine Motor Skills

Fun on a Shoestring

Games with Sounds

Growing Things

ICT

Investigations

Junk Music

Kitchen Stuff

Language Fun

Light and Shadow

Listening

Living Things

Look and Listen

Making Books and Cards

Maps and Plans

Making Poetry

Mark Making

Maths Activities

Maths from Stories

Maths Outdoors

Maths Songs and Games

Messy Play

Minibeast Hotels

Music

Nursery Rhymes

Outdoor Play

Outside in All Weathers

Parachute Play

Persona Dolls

Phonics

Playground Games

Prop Boxes for Role Play

Props for Writing

Puppet Making

Puppets in Stories

Resistant Materials

Role Play

Sand and Water

Science through Art

Scissor Skills

Sewing and Weaving

Small World Play

Sound Ideas

Special Days

Stories Fom Around The World

Storyboards

Storytelling

Seasons

Time and Money

Time and Place

Traditional Tales

Treasure Baskets

Treasureboxes

Tuff Spot Activities

Washing Lines

Writing

Woodwork

All available from
www.bloomsbury.com/featherstone